Contents

Dear Friends,

I am Reva. My twin sister Sarayu and I love travelling. This time we will take you on an exciting journey to visit the most amazing and spectacular regions in the northern, southern, eastern, and western parts of our country. The regions we shall travel to are not only beautiful, but also very interesting. These places are amazing creations of nature that are fascinating and mysterious too. That is why they are known as The Natural Wonders of India.

Not only will we have fun, but we will also learn about the exciting stories behind each of these wonders. The stories of our travels will help you understand what a Natural Wonder is, why it is there, how we can take care of it, and much more.

Together, we shall:

- Unravel the mystery behind the Magnetic Hills
- Enjoy the sight of models of dinosaurs and a display of their eggs in Indroda Dinosaur and Fossil Park
- See the beauty of the emerald-green water of Lonar Crater Lake created by a meteorite hit, and so on

The Natural Wonders of India

Vijaylakshmi Nagaraj

Magnetic Hi[ll]

Majuli Island

Indroda Dinosaur and Fossil Park

Mawsmai Cave

teri

The Energy and Resources Institute

An imprint of The Energy and Resources Institute

First published in 2013 by
The Energy and Resources Institute
TERI Press
Darbari Seth Block, IHC Complex, Lodhi Road, New Delhi 110 003, India
Tel. 2468 2100/4150 4900, Fax: 2468 2144/2468 2145
India +91 ▪ Delhi (0)11
Email: teripress@teri.res.in ▪ Website: http://bookstore.teriin.org

ISBN 978-81-7993-449-4

Publishing Head: Anupama Jauhry
Editorial and Production Teams: Rupak Ghosh, Himanshi Sharma;
Aman Sachdeva
Design and Illustration Teams: Santosh Gautam, Vijay Kumar;
Yatindra Kumar, Vijay Nipane
Image Researcher: Shilpa Mohan

Printed and bound in India

This book is printed on recycled paper.

Before you turn the pages and join us in our voyage of discovery and wonder, we want to bring to your attention a matter of concern. During our travels, we have observed that animals and plants living in these beautiful places are slowly dying. We have already lost many of them that we may never see again. There are others that are on the verge of disappearing forever.

UNESCO has taken the responsibility of taking care of some of these places by making them World Heritage sites, but don't you think it would be great if we could also help in preserving and taking care of all these places in our own little way? Then our country will remain ever beautiful.

Come, join us in our exciting journey through these wonderlands of India, and let us ensure that we keep their beauty alive!

Cheers,
Reva and Sarayu

Pangong Tso

Colonel Ram had planned an exciting summer vacation for his twin daughters Reva and Sarayu. The girls with their mother joined him in Leh, where he was posted.

"Leh, the capital of Ladakh, is a high plateau and is also called **Shangri-la**. It means a calm, beautiful place", said Ram.
"No running, jumping, or hopping till you get used to the altitude", said Anju.
"Why, Ma?" asked the twins.

"The air here has less oxygen. So, you can get **breathless** easily", she replied.
"Tourists are asked to rest for the first 24 hours so that they don't suffer from high-altitude sickness", their father added.
"What kind of sickness is that?" Reva asked.

"You get headaches and have difficulty breathing. Also, you may not be able to sleep and eat", Col. Ram explained.

Early next morning, they left by road to see a beautiful Natural **Wonder**.
"Where are we going, Papa?" Sarayu asked.
"Pangong Tso", her father replied.
"And what is that?" asked Reva.
"*Tso* means lake and Pangong Tso is a 130 km-long lake, located at a height of 14,500 ft. One-third of the lake is in India and the rest extends into western Tibet", he explained.
The six-hour journey, along a winding road, took them across Chang La, **one** of the **highest** motorable roads, to reach the Lake.

"Ma, the water is blue and suddenly it turns green, purple, violet, orange, and red, just like a **rainbow**!" exclaimed Sarayu.

"These colours are created by the reflection of the Sun's rays on the lake", her mother explained.

"Keep an eye on the sandy area around the waters. You might spot a yak, marmot, wild ass, or a fox, if you are lucky", said Col. Ram, while adding,

"Look! A black-necked Siberian crane. This is a **migratory** bird."

Reva collected pebbles of all sizes and shapes from the lake side, while Sarayu sketched the beautiful surroundings.

"We will have something exciting to tell all our friends when we go back", chorused the twin sisters.

After returning to Leh at nightfall, the beauty and wonder of Pangong Tso remained with them.

Magnetic Hill

The famous Magnetic Hill in Ladakh was the next destination for the twins and their parents.

"Magnetic Hill! How can a hill be like a magnet, Papa?" asked Sarayu with curiosity.

"Well, it's not really a magnet", said Col. Ram. "But it is really **extraordinary**."

"That sounds interesting", exclaimed Reva.

"The Magnetic Hill lies 14,000 ft above the sea level", said Col. Ram, as he continued driving towards the Magnetic Hill. "It is

30 km away from Leh town on the Kargil Highway, towards the west of the Indus river", he added as he drove his jeep ahead.

Soon they reached a yellow board. It read:
Magnetic Hill — The phenomenon that defies gravity. Park your vehicle in the box marked with white paint on the road.

Col. Ram drove the jeep into the white square and switched off the engine.
What happened next left the twins dumbstruck.
The jeep slowly started moving on its own, even though its engine was off!
Still inside the jeep, Col. Ram looked back at his daughters, whose mouths

were open wide in surprise.
"It seems as if a magnet is pulling our jeep", said Anju.

"We want to get out and see the **jeep going uphill** once more, Mumma", requested the twins, to which their parents agreed. As soon as they got off the jeep, Sarayu promptly clicked a photograph of the yellow board.

Col. Ram switched off the engine, and once again the jeep slowly began moving.

"How does this happen, Papa?" asked Reva.

"Well, it appears as if the jeep is moving uphill against the force of **gravity**. This is actually an optical illusion and that is the mystery of the Magnetic Hill", explained Col. Ram.

"What is an **optical illusion**?" queried Sarayu.

"It means something that looks very different from what it actually is", said Col. Ram.

"And gravity?" Reva chipped in.
"There is a force, which pulls all of us to the centre of the Earth. It is called gravity. This gravity is what keeps our feet on the ground", explained Col. Ram.
"Would all of us float otherwise?" Reva interrupted.
"That would be fun!" exclaimed Sarayu.
Their parents smiled at them.
"Life would be difficult if there was no gravity, because we and everything around us would be flying", added Anju.
"Oh!" said Sarayu with a big sigh.
"I am glad I have my feet on the ground", giggled Reva, stomping her feet.

"That was an awesome mystery, Papa."
"Amazing Magnetic Hill!" said Sarayu, chuckling with joy.

Krem Mawsmai

For their next outing, a school trip during the Dussehra holidays, the twins visited Meghalaya, also called the "Abode of Clouds". Sarayu, Reva, and their classmates were all very excited at the idea of **exploring** the famous caves of Meghalaya.

"Don't forget to note down and draw what you see. It will be useful when you do your holiday homework", said Ms Roy, their Science teacher.

"Meghalaya has many underground passages that run in and out of the hills. It has several caves and caverns too", said the guide. Meanwhile, Ms Roy ensured that all the students had clipped their identity cards to their sweaters.

"What are caverns?" asked Reva.

"They are large, dark caves", explained the guide.

"These are natural **underground** spaces", he added.

"So, is it scary inside?" asked Sarayu.

"No, don't be afraid. They are Nature's work of art, a beautiful natural wonder", said Ms Roy.

"Over 1,000 caves like these have been discovered in Meghalaya", said the guide.

"How are they formed?" asked Reva.

"Caves are usually formed from sedimentary rocks, especially limestone", Ms Roy replied.

"Sedimentary rocks? **Limestone**?" repeated the students, a little confused.

"Thousands of years ago, pieces of rocks containing calcium were washed away by water and wind. They gathered in one place on top of each other and gradually became hard. They often extended deep into the ground", explained Ms Roy.

"Oh!" chorused the students.
"The most famous caves are in the Khasi Hills. Shella, Mawsynram, Nongjri, Pynursla, and Langrin are other areas famous for their caves", said the guide. "We are going to see Krem Mawsmai, which is near Cherrapunji in the Khasi Hills and close to the village of Mawsmai."
"What is *Krem*?" asked Sarayu.
"*Krem* is the Khasi word for cave", he explained.

"Though the entry is narrow, the cave is pretty large inside", said the guide as he led them in.
The lamps lit inside the cave helped everyone move ahead.

"Just look at the stalactites", pointed Ms Roy.
"They look so pretty!" said Sarayu chuckling with joy.
"What are they?" asked Reva.
"When drops of water seep into the cave through cracks, they come in contact with the air inside. They later harden, forming little rings on the roof of the cave", explained the guide. "Over tens of thousands of years, they become long, pointed, stick-like structures hanging downwards from the ceiling."

"And what are these cones on the ground?" asked Reva.
"They are stalagmites", said Ms Roy.

The children were happy to have learnt about such interesting things inside the cave.

"It's so cold here. I'm glad that we were told to wear our sweaters", said Reva.

"Is this the longest cave?" asked Sarayu.

"No. Krem Liat Prah-Um Im-Labit System is India's longest cave and it is located in the Jaintia Hills. We will visit it some other day", said Ms Roy.

"It is all nature's work. Look at the space inside the cave. It is like a big hall", said the guide.

"Come on children! This is the right place for a photograph", said Ms Roy.

"CHEESE", said all the students as the camera flashed.

Majuli Island

On a map of India, Sarayu and her cousin Aayush were trying to decide where to go for their next holiday. Aayush had come down from Bangkok to spend his October vacation with Sarayu and Reva.

"How about visiting an island?" asked Anju.
"Which one?" questioned Aayush.

Anju pointed at Majuli Island in **Assam**, on the map.
"So, it's in the middle of a big river. Will there be a boat ride too, Uncle Ram?" asked Aayush, bubbling with excitement.
"Wait and watch!" said Col. Ram with a smile.
Next day, the family was ready for the trip, with their bags packed.
"From Shillong, we'll drive to Jorhat in Upper Assam. Then, it is 20 km to reach Nimatighat, a *ghat* on the banks of River Brahmaputra, before

hopping onto a ferry to Majuli", Col. Ram explained to the kids. Crossing the river, they reached Kamalabari where their guide Mr Mahanta, a historian, was waiting for them.

"Majuli is a **pollution-free island**. The Indian government is requesting UNESCO to recognize it as a World Heritage Site", he said. "What is a World Heritage Site?" asked Reva. Mr Mahanta explained, "It is an area looked after by UNESCO. It can be a mountain, lake, island, desert, forest, building, and so on. These are places of wonder, culturally or naturally. Majuli is one such place. It is rich in **biodiversity**".
"Biodiversity?" enquired Aayush.
"It means Majuli is home to a variety of animals, plants, and birds. There are over 1,000 different types of trees, creepers, flowers, and

orchids here. Both local and **migratory birds**, such as the stork, pelican, and the Siberian crane are found here", Mr Mahanta said. "Let's go for a walk around the island."

Photo: Ganesh Jayaraman

"Majuli has 243 villages, and the people here mostly belong to the Mishing and Deori tribes", he said.

"Those village houses look interesting", said Sarayu, pointing to some houses at a distance. "Why are they built on **bamboo stilts**?"

"These stilts prevent flood waters from entering homes", Mr Mahanta replied.

"Hey! There's a monastery", shouted Aayush in excitement.

"I'll take you there", said Mr Mahanta.

"We call a monastery *Satra*. This one is the *Vaishnava Satra*. Various festivals are celebrated here."

"Which is the most famous festival?" asked Reva.

"The *Rasleela* during the *Karthik Purnima* in November", he replied. Later, he took the family to the other *Satras*, where they saw collections of weapons, antiques, and other artistic items.

"At the *Satras*, experts teach dance, music, drama, and art and craft. The women weave colourful and traditional clothes and a special quilt called 'jim'. The handloom products of this place are famous all over the world", he explained.

Sarayu and Aayush were busy clicking photographs, while Reva was watching pottery and mask making.

"Come on, children! Let's go for a cruise down the river and watch some birds", Col. Ram called out. Soon it was time to leave.

"Thank you, Mr Mahanta! My friends in Bangkok will love to hear about this amazing natural wonder", said Aayush as he shook hands with the guide before parting.

5 Alappuzha

Reva and Sarayu's school was celebrating **Grandparents Day**. All the students' grandparents had been invited to speak about one natural wonder of India of their choice.

"Meet my grandma", said Vivek to his classmates. "Her name is Asha and she has come from Kerala."

Asha smiled as all the children eagerly waited for her to begin her story.

"Hello, children! I come from a place in Kerala called Alappuzha", said Asha. "Alappuzha, also known as **Alleppey**, is famous for its canals, which **zigzag** through the town.

You can sail through the canals in different types of boats — from small country boats to speedboats and even houseboats where tourists can stay."

"You mean a boat that is actually a house?" cried Sarayu with excitement. Asha smiled and nodded.

"How do people live with all that water around them?" asked Reva.
"Villagers staying on the banks of the canals use their boats to carry out their daily activities", explained Asha.
"Does that mean instead of cars, people use boats to travel in Alappuzha?" queried Reva.
"Yes, my dear", Asha smiled. "In fact, Alappuzha is also called the 'Venice of the East'. **Kuttanad**, the rice bowl of Kerala, is another famous place in Alappuzha. Here, you can see miles of paddy fields. Did you know in some areas of Kuttanad, farming is done about 40 ft below sea level? This kind of farming is done in only a few other places in the world."
"Flocks of parrots flying across paddy fields and a large number of ducks swimming across the backwaters are a common sight", she added.

"When is the best time to visit Alappuzha?" asked Sarayu.
"Well, Kerala is very hot and humid during summers. So, the best time to visit Alappuzha is during August-September or February-March", replied Grandma Asha.
"It must be really fun staying in a houseboat!" exclaimed Sarayu.

"Oh, yes. We call houseboats *kettuvallam*. You can relax and have a great time while staying in these houseboats", she replied.
"Tell us more about Alappuzha", chorused all the students.
"Alappuzha has thick palm groves and ancient, tall lighthouses. Its backwater journeys take you through emerald-green landscapes, tall coconut groves, temples, monuments, churches, and villages along the banks. Make sure you do not miss the **Punnamada lake**", said Asha.

"What is special about this lake, grandma?" asked one of the students.

"This is where the legendary **Nehru Trophy Boat Race** takes place on the second Saturday of August every year. People from all over the world come to see this famous boat race", she replied.

"Can we visit you in Alappuzha, grandma Asha?" asked Sarayu, resting her chin on her palms.

"Of course! You are all welcome", she said and took some pictures out of her bag. "Take a look at these photographs of Alappuzha and Kuttanad." The students chorused, "Thank you, grandma Asha".

Cardamom Hills

"Welcome to the Cardamom Hills, Sarayu and Reva", said Ms Wilson as the van in which they were travelling came to a halt. Ms Wilson was Anju's friend. She had organized this special summer holiday trip for the twins.

"The Cardamom Hills are a part of the Western Ghats. These Hills are 2,637 m high and extend across Kerala and Tamil Nadu", said Ms Wilson.
"Does it mean they are very high?" asked Reva.

"Yes, Reva", replied Ms Wilson. "Anaimudi in Kerala is the highest peak in southern India. It stands 2,695 m tall and overlooks the Eravikulam National Park", she added.

"Does *Anaimudi* mean anything? Because in Tamil *Anai* means elephant", questioned Sarayu.

"Yes, it does. *Mudi* means forehead, so *Anaimudi* means **Elephant's forehead**", Ms Wilson replied.
"These dense forests are home to many endangered animals, such as the Nilgiri langurs, macaques, leopards, and tigers", she added.
"What are endangered animals?" asked Reva.

"Animals whose numbers are decreasing are called **endangered** animals. Such animals face threat, because they are either hunted or they lose their homes when forests are cut down. If we do not take care of them, they will soon disappear forever. So forest rangers ensure the safety of such animals", explained Ms Wilson.
"Now we are at the base of the Cardamom Hills, in the Thattekad Bird Sanctuary. It is also known as Dr Salim Ali Bird Sanctuary. Dr Salim Ali was a famous ornithologist", said Ms Wilson as she held Reva's hand.

"**Ornithologist**?" asked the twins.

"A person who studies birds and knows a lot about them", said
Ms Wilson. "Listen carefully to the sound of birds."
The twins were quietly enjoying the melodious call of birds.
"Next, we are going to see the Periyar Wildlife Sanctuary. It has an
artificial lake."
"Does that mean it's not a natural lake like Pangong Tso?" asked Reva.
"That's correct", replied Ms Wilson. "Elephants, gaurs, tigers, Sambar
deer, and many other animals come to this lake. If we are lucky, we might
spot them."
A little later, she asked, "Children, do you know about a very special Indian
spice called cardamom?"

"Yes. Mummy puts it in rice pudding", said Reva. "She also adds it in
her tea", added Sarayu.
"Come, we'll walk around the Cardamom Hills and you will actually see
cardamom growing", said Ms Wilson. "Then an elephant ride."
"Really?" shouted the twins in excitement.
Soon Sarayu, Reva, and Ms Wilson were enjoying an elephant ride through
the tea and coffee plantations on the hill slopes. They saw pepper plants

with clusters of pepper.

"Now you know that we not only get cardamom from Cardamom Hills… "
said Ms Wilson. " …but tea, coffee, and pepper too", chorused the twins.
"Take a deep breath and smell the spices", she said. The twins did
the same happily and thanked Ms Wilson for bringing them to the
Cardamom Hills.
Soon they were ready to return home.
"Oh, I wish I could stay here longer", exclaimed Sarayu.
"We'll come here again", assured Ms Wilson.

Rann of Kutch

The twins, who had never seen the Rann of Kutch, were looking forward to this trip with Aunt Meher. Travelling in Meher's jalopy helped them see this huge **salt marsh** in all its beauty. Introducing them to Kutch, Meher said, "This large flat ground, which is shining in the Sun, is actually covered with salt and minerals".

"Does Rann of Kutch mean we are supposed to run here, aunty?" asked Sarayu.

"No, my dear!" said Meher, laughing. Reva giggled too. "*Rann* is a Hindi word, which means desert. It lies in Gujarat", she explained.

"This region remains hot during the day and cold at night. Here summers are very hot, while winters are really cold", she added.

"Oh, I am glad we are here in December and not in the summers", said Sarayu.

"And there is the small… umm… and big Rann of Kutch. Right, aunty?" asked Reva.

"It's not 'small' and 'big', but the Little and Great Rann of Kutch, dear! They were originally extensions of the Arabian Sea till they got cut off", said Meher. "The Great Rann of Kutch is in the north and the Little Rann is towards its east."
The twins were all ears.
"Do you want to know how the local people here make salt?" asked Meher.
"How?" queried Sarayu.

"This place has salt water. The locals make a small pit and leave the water to dry in the hot Sun. After a few days, grains of salt are formed", described Meher.

"During the rainy season, the low-lying land along the coast gets flooded and the tides deposit mud. Such places are called mudflats. When the tide comes, they become wet. But during summer, they are dry. Then, all you can see are the Banni grasslands and dry thorny scrubs. There are hardly any trees", she explained.

"What are Banni grasslands?" asked Reva.

"They are areas with grass, on which cattle graze", explained Meher.

"Look!" said Meher at a herd of animals in the distance. "Can you see the Asiatic Wild Ass over there?"

"Yes, aunty!" shouted the twins.

"Rann of Kutch is the only place in the world where you can find this endangered animal", she said. "You can also see the **Blackbuck** here, which is an endangered animal too."

As they drove on, they saw a flock of **flamingos**.
"This place is the India's largest breeding ground for flamingos", explained Meher. "Every year, they come here in large numbers."
While Reva was busy clicking pictures, Sarayu began sketching the scene besides paying attention to what Aunt Meher was saying.
"The salty mudflats of Rann cover a large area. Many varieties of birds come here during the winters", said Meher. "The government is making sure that this place is protected. Cutting of trees is not allowed here."
"We will spread this message to our friends and relatives in Bengaluru", said Reva. "We'll make sure both of us and everyone around us take care of the environment", added Sarayu with a big smile.

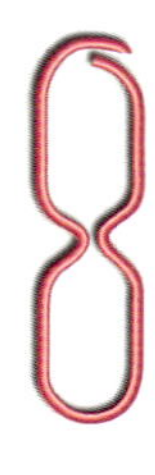

Indroda Dinosaur and Fossil Park

"Aunty, are you really taking us to see a Dinosaur Park?" asked Reva. "Yes! Today, you shall see the most extraordinary park located in Gandhinagar in Gujarat", replied Aunt Meher.

"When we saw the movie *Jurassic Park* in school, we got so scared, because we thought the dinosaurs will actually come to eat us up. Then our teacher told us that dinosaurs do not exist anymore", said Sarayu, who was a little afraid at the thought of visiting a dinosaur park.

"What your teacher has told you is true", Meher assured the twins.

"The Indroda Dinosaur and Fossil Park is unique. In fact, more children came to see this park after watching *Jurassic Park*, because they were curious to know about dinosaurs", explained Meher.

While Sarayu breathed a sigh of relief, Reva asked, "What is so special about this dinosaur park, aunty?"

"You'll find out when you go there."

Within a few hours, they reached the Indroda Dinosaur and Fossil Park. It was spread over a large area on either sides of the Sabarmati river.

"This park, which is on the western bank of the Sabarmati, is the Indroda Nature Park. The one on the eastern bank is the Wilderness Park", explained Meher as she parked her jalopy.

"Do you know why this park exists at this site?" The twins shook their head to say, "No".

She explained, "That's because the world's second-largest collection of dinosaur eggs was found here".

Soon, they entered the park.

"Wow! This is wonderful! Look at the life-sized models of dinosaurs!" exclaimed Reva.

"Hey! This one's called Pterodactyl", shouted Sarayu while pointing towards a huge model.

"It is a famous dinosaur", said Meher.

"This place looks like the Indian Jurassic Park", said Reva, giggling with joy.
"Come, I will show you some fossils of dinosaur bones and eggs too", said Meher.

"The plaque says that the **fossils** are 65 million years old", exclaimed Reva as she looked at the eggs.
Meher said, "One million means 1000, 000", while Reva interrupted saying, "Oh my God! So, 65 million years old means very, very old!"
"Yes, my dear", said Meher. "Do you know this is the only dinosaur museum in the country?" she added.
The twins could not control their excitement when they saw huge

skeletons of a **blue whale** and other sea animals.
"I am curious to know what happened to all these animals", asked Reva.
"Scientists have not been able to figure out exactly why they disappeared", said Meher. "It could be climate change, some deadly disease, or a meteorite hit."

"Aunty, we should protect the animals that we have today otherwise they will become extinct too", said the twins in unison.

"Of course, my dear!" said Meher. "Our animals are part of our heritage. We all should be sensitive about them."
On this note, they began walking towards the car to go back home.

9 Lonar Crater Lake

Sarayu and Reva were really lucky that Aunt Meher, their mother's best friend, loved travelling and knew a lot of exciting places. Driving her red jalopy, with the twins seated at the back, she was off to the small village of Lonar in Buldana district of Maharashtra. It was just four-and-a-half hours away from the famous Ajanta Caves, which they had recently visited.

"This place is believed to be **50,000 years old**", said Meher. "Really?" exclaimed Sarayu with surprise.

"Yes, scientists have recently found evidence that a **meteorite** from Mars could have created this lake", explained Meher. "What is a meteorite?" asked Reva. "It is a huge ball of fire that comes from outer space and enters the Earth's atmosphere. Meteors usually burn up completely in the sky.

But sometimes, they reach the Earth's surface, forming craters as they hit the ground", clarified Meher.
"Oh! That is so interesting", uttered the twins.

"Did you know this is the third largest **crater** in the world?" asked Meher. "It was discovered in 1823 by a British officer J E Alexander. The meteorite that created this lake broke into three pieces, forming three craters. The other two craters also formed lakes – Ganesh lake and Ambar lake – both of which have dried. Now, let us see what is written on this board", said Meher.

"*The only natural hyper-velocity impact crater in* **basaltic rock** *in the world.*"
"What does that mean?" asked the twins.
"Simply that the meteorite was traveling really fast. It struck the Earth's surface here and created this natural, saltwater lake", explained Meher.
"The stones found in this lake are similar to those found in the craters on Moon."

"That's wonderful to know!" exclaimed the twins.

"And there is a **mystery** about this lake too. It always remains full. This is because a stream flows into it, but no water ever flows out", said Meher.

"It looks so blue and cool", exclaimed Reva. "And the forest around the lake is full of trees and flowers. It is so pretty", added Sarayu.

"Nearby there are temples. One of them has a sculpture, which tells us about the formation of this crater", said Meher. "Gazelles, langurs, peacocks, and many other birds are found here. Now I want to tell you something that is of serious concern. This lovely lake is getting polluted."

"**How**?" chorused the twins.

"Pesticides and fertilizers used in the area surrounding the lake are making the waters dirty and unfit for drinking", replied Meher. "Many people **bathe** in the lake's waters and pollute it too."

"Aunty, the polluted water will harm the animals, who come to drink here, no?" asked Reva.

"Yes. So people have to make sure that the lake is clean. All those who come to see this beautiful place should see to it that the beauty of this natural wonder is not spoiled", said Meher.

Reva and Sarayu held her hands and looked at the lake, while the Sun was setting.

10 Siachen Glacier

Sarayu, Reva, and their cousins Rani and Krishna had gone to spend their summer vacation with their grandparents. One day, they found an old photograph.

"Reva, that's Grandpa wearing a huge coat, dark glasses, a big fur cap, and large boots!" said Sarayu excitedly.

Grandpa, a retired **Army Officer**, was relaxing on his favourite rocking chair when the four children rushed in.

"Grandpa, we want to know about this photograph!" said Reva.

"Where was it taken?" asked Krishna.

"Story, Grandpa", requested Rani, the youngest of them all, as she made herself comfortable on his lap while others sat on the carpet around him.

"This photograph was taken on my first trip to the Siachen Glacier in the 1980s", he said with a smile. "Siachen lies at the northernmost tip of India in the Ladakh region of Jammu and Kashmir. The glacier is about 70 km long. It is the longest **glacier** in the Karakoram range of the Himalayas. It is also the second-longest glacier outside of the Poles."

"What is a glacier, Grandpa? Please tell me!" Sarayu was full of questions.

"Glacier means a slow-moving river of ice", replied Grandpa.

"A river of ice? That's a lot of ice, Grandpa", exclaimed Reva.

Grandpa laughed aloud and said, "Yes. This river starts at Indira Col and empties into the Nubra river. Every year, about 10–12 m of snow falls in this region".

"How much **snow** is that?" asked Krishna.

"As tall as a two-storey building. Right, Grandpa?" asked Reva.

"Yes", replied Grandpa, while adding, "With extreme sub-zero temperatures dipping to minus 50 degrees Centigrade, no one lives in the Glacier region."

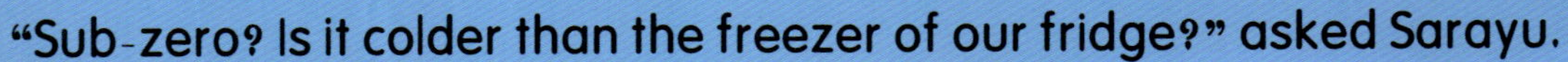

"Sub-zero? Is it colder than the freezer of our fridge?" asked Sarayu.

"Much, much colder. In fact, my **toothpaste** used to freeze. I had to put it in hot water to squeeze the paste out", said Grandpa while the children were listening attentively. "I had to wear special clothes, as you can see in the photograph, to keep myself warm. We had to be very careful of frostbite, breathlessness, chilblain, and other problems."
"But where did you live?" asked Rani.
"At first, we stayed in tents in the main camp, near the end of the Glacier.

Then, when we shifted to the higher areas, we **tunneled** into the snow and made a cave-like living space", explained Grandpa.
"The chilly winds, snow storms, and avalanches made it very tough for us. We had to first melt the ice and then make tea", he added.
"And what about food?" asked Reva.
"How did it reach you?" enquired Krishna.

"Well, sometimes I did not feel like eating. So, we were given special kinds of energy food and chocolates", replied Grandpa. "Usually, food was brought in by **helicopters**."

"Can we visit the Glacier?" queried Krishna.
"People on mountaineering expeditions are allowed to go. You can become a **mountaineer** when you grow up and visit this amazing natural wonder called Siachen Glacier", said Grandpa.
As soon as Rani heard this, she uttered, "I will become a mountaineer, when I grow up!" and everybody broke into laughter.

Meanwhile, Reva and Sarayu were already wondering which natural wonder they should visit next...

Did You Know?

Pangong Tso lake is shared by India and China. It is the highest saltwater lake in the world.

The **Magnetic Hill** is also known as a gravity hill. There are magnetic hills in numerous other locations of the world too, Canada being one of them.

Nearly 1200 **caves** have been reported in Meghalaya, of which Synrang Pamiang, located in Jaintia Hills, is the deepest. The world's biggest cave lies in the jungles of Vietnam. Known as the Son Doong, it measures 262 X 262 ft in most places.

Majuli is the largest river Island in India. It is feared that due to erosion, the river island might drown and disappear in the next 15–20 years.

Alappuzha means the land between the sea and network of rivers flowing into it. The most amazing fact about the Kettuvallam houseboat is that not a single nail is used in the making of this boat; it is made by tying pieces of wood.

The **Cardamom Hills** are home to many tribal people, who work in the tea gardens to earn their livelihood.

Kutch is the largest district in terms of area in India. This place is extremely vulnerable to earthquakes, drought, and cyclones.

Some of the eggs found in the **Indroda Dinosaur and Fossil Park** are as big as cannon balls.

Scientists have estimated that the meteorite that created the **Lonar Crater lake** was travelling at a speed of 25 km per second. It was recently discovered that a bacterium found on Mars, named *Bacillus odyssey*, was found inside the lake.

Sia means rose and *Chun* means an object found in abundance; **Siachen** means the land of roses. Siachen is home to rare species like snow leopard, brown bear, and ibex.

Mapping is Fun!

Can you identify the natural wonders that we have just visited on the map of India? To make it easier, one example has been done for you.

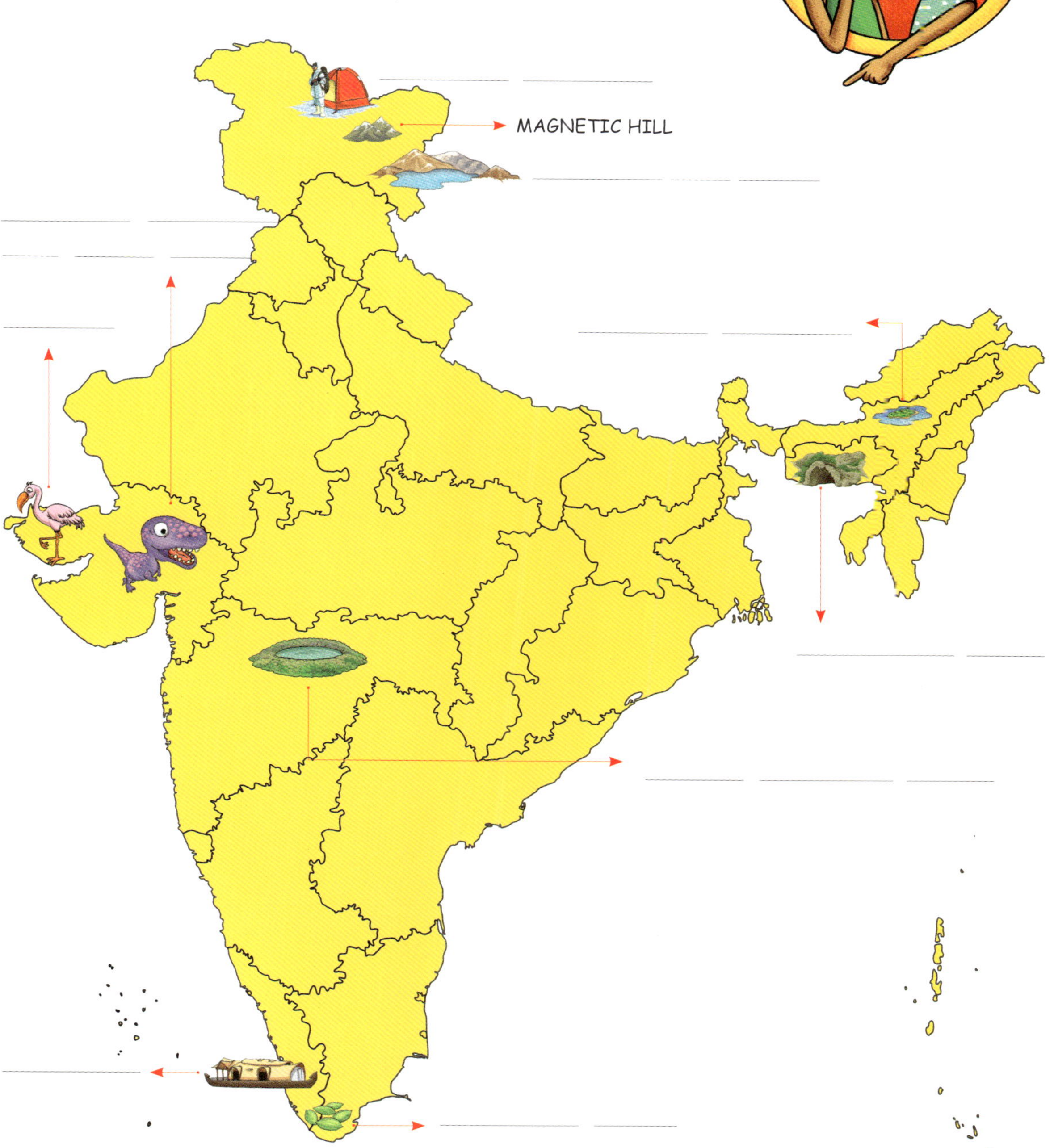

47

Words to Remember

Avalanche:	a large mass of snow and ice or rocks sliding swiftly and suddenly down a mountain side
Backwaters:	part of a river not reached by the current, where water remains stagnant
Banni grasslands:	dry grasslands
Basaltic rock:	a hard dark volcanic rock
Biodiversity:	a large variety of animals, plants, birds, and insects in a particular habitat/area
Cavern:	a large cave
Chilblain:	inflammation or swelling of hands and feet caused by exposure to extreme cold
Fossil:	remains of a prehistoric animal or plant preserved in the Earth and hardened like a rock
Glacier:	a huge mass of ice slowly flowing down a slope or valley
Gravity:	the force that attracts bodies towards the centre of Earth
Handloom:	weaving cloth by hand using a loom (textile machinery)
Migratory:	birds and animals moving from one area to another at particular times of the year
Monastery:	the residence of a community of monks
Monument:	a building that is preserved because of its historical importance to a country
Mudflats:	coastal wetlands that are formed when mud is deposited by tides
Phenomenon:	a fact, an occurrence
Plaque:	a piece of stone or metal with writing on it fixed on a wall as an ornament or memorial
Plateau:	an area of land that is flat and raised much higher than the surrounding areas
Sedimentary rocks:	type of rocks that are formed by the deposition of sediment transported by water on the Earth's surface
Velocity:	speed